The Let's Talk Library™

Let's Talk About
Living with a Grandparent

Susan Kent

The Rosen Publishing Group's
PowerKids Press™
New York

To Donald and Virginia Kent (and Vera and Peter Cakars in memoriam)—
the greatest of grandparents.

Published in 2000 by The Rosen Publishing Group, Inc.
29 East 21st Street, New York, NY 10010

First Edition

Book design: Erin McKenna

Photo Illustrations by Debra L. Rothenberg

Kent, Susan, 1942—
    Let's talk about living with a grandparent / by Susan Kent.
        p.   cm.—(The let's talk library)
    Includes index.
    Summary: Discusses various reasons for living with a grandparent, the benefits of such an arrangement, and how to help out at home.
    ISBN 0-8239-5421-8 (lib. bdg.)
    1. Grandparent and child—Juvenile literature. [1. Grandparents.] I. Title. II. Title: Let us talk about living with a grandparent. III. Series.
BF723.G68K46 1998
306.874'5—dc21
                                          98-44975
                                               CIP
                                             AC

Manufactured in the United States of America

Table of Contents

Maria

Maria has a big family. Mama, Papa, Aunt Tanya, Grandma, Grandpa, Maria, her sister, and her three cousins all live together.

While Maria's parents work at the family store, Grandma and Grandpa take care of the children. Maria helps out by watching her sister and little cousins while Grandma cooks. After dinner, she helps dry the dishes while Grandma washes. When Maria finishes her homework, she helps out in the store, too. Her favorite job is piling up the oranges.

◀ *Maria likes to help her grandma. After dinner they wash and dry the dishes together.*

Children and Grandparents

You might live with your grandparents for a little while or all your life. Your whole family may live together to help each other, like Maria's does. A grandparent may move in with you if he or she cannot live alone.

You may go to live with your grandparents if your parents travel a lot or get a job far away. Maybe your parents are sick, or they are having problems and need to do things on their own for a while. Many children live with their grandparents for many different reasons.

It can be a very exciting time when your grandparent comes to live with you. ▶

Living with Grandparents

It can be hard when you first move in with your grandparents. They probably don't do everything the way your parents did. It is not easy to get used to a new place and different rules. You may be sad, or angry at your parents for leaving. It is O.K. to feel upset if your parents cannot be there. Remember, though, that your parents and grandparents care about you and are trying to make things better for you.

◀ Sometimes grandparents have different house rules than your parents. It's a good idea to talk about the rules together.

Grandparents Are Special

If you live with a grandparent, you are lucky. Grandparents are special people. They took care of and raised your parents when they were young. Now they love and care for you. They are **experienced** and can teach you the many things they know. They can help you to understand the world you live in. Your grandparents may have time to spend with you when other people are busy.

Grandparents can be a lot of fun. Enjoy the time you spend with them.

This girl teaches her grandmother how to play her favorite game. ▶

Richard

Richard lives alone with his grandma. His grandpa and his parents died when he was a baby, so Richard doesn't remember them. He loves his grandma and is happy living with her.

Richard's grandma is the best singer in her church's choir. She is teaching Richard to sing and play the piano. Sometimes they sing together. Richard has already sung in his school's chorus. He hopes that he will be as good a singer as his grandma.

◀ *Richard practices his singing. He wants to make his grandma proud.*

Grandparents Have a Hard Job

It is a hard job for grandparents to raise a second family. They have already done it once and may not have planned to do it again. Since they are older now, they might not have as much energy as when they raised your mom or dad. They might have to work at another job as well as take care of you. When they come home, they might feel tired.

Though things can be hard sometimes, your grandparents love you and want to take care of you.

This boy gets a cold glass of water for his grandpa after a long day. ▶

How to Help Grandparents

The best thing you can do to help your grandparents is to show them you care about them. You can draw them a picture or pick them some flowers or pretty autumn leaves. Read them a story you wrote in school. When you see that your grandparents are tired, ask what you can do to help. You could go to the store or just play quietly. You could help clean the house or wash the dishes. Your grandparents will **appreciate** your help.

◀ *Saying "I love you" will make your grandparents' day.*

17

How Grandparents Help You

Your grandparents can love you and take care of you. They can feed you and keep you warm. They can also give you advice and share their **wisdom** with you. They can help you with your schoolwork and watch you play ball or act in your school play. They can take you to the park and to the zoo. Grandparents can be there for you when you need them, in good times and in bad times.

This boy is home sick, but he feels better knowing his grandpa is taking good care of him. ▶

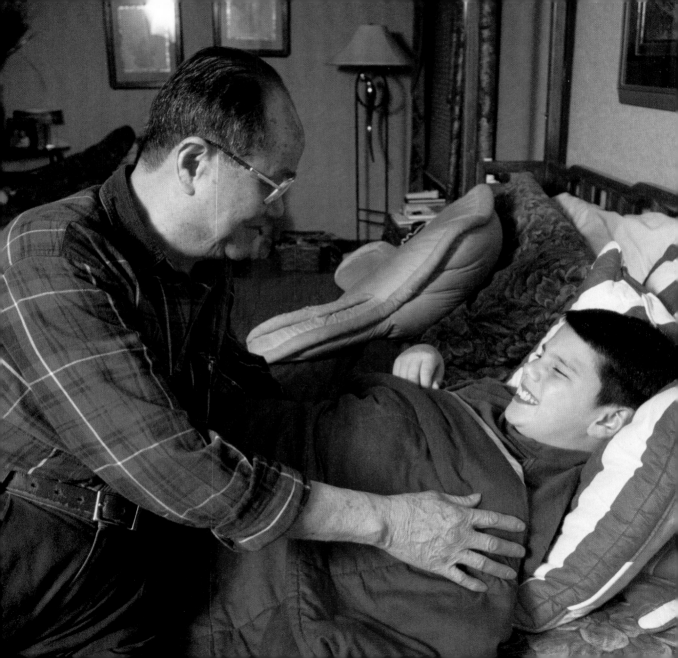

Gary and Sally

Gary and Sally live with their Pop-Pop and Nana. Both of their parents are in the army far away.

Pop-Pop is a fisherman. He is teaching Gary and Sally his secret recipe for fish stew. First they go with Pop-Pop in his boat to catch the fish. Then they pick tomatoes with Nana in her garden. Nana is a **potter**. She teaches them how to make bowls out of clay that they dig from the riverbank. After they make the stew, they eat it out of their bowls.

◀ *Fishing is just one way to spend special time with your grandparents.*

Family History

Grandparents are like living **ancestors**. They can teach you about your family history. They can tell you what the world was like when they were young and how it has changed. They can tell you about the lives of *their* parents and grandparents. They can also tell you funny stories about your parents when they were little. Learning your family history helps you understand where you came from and who you are.

You are lucky to live with a grandparent. You get extra help and extra love.

22

Glossary

ancestors (AN-ses-terz) Family members who lived before you.

appreciate (a-PREE-she-ate) To be thankful for.

experienced (ik-SPIR-ee-enst) When a person has knowledge or skill gained by doing or seeing things.

potter (PAH-ter) A person who makes pots, dishes, bowls, or other things, out of earth or clay.

wisdom (WIZ-dum) Being wise, knowing a lot about something through doing or seeing things.

Index